Education
The key to a better future

By

Dr. Dennis V. Burke

There is an invisible hand guiding each pursuit of a win-win solution

CONTENTS

CONTENTS

INTRODUCTION

Education is a fundamental part of human development and progress. A good education produces benefits beyond the individual to our society. It has two functional features -learning and teaching. Effective educators understand that learning and teaching overlap and are inseparable. Hence the axiom, "By teaching, we learn." Education includes acquiring knowledge and skills, fostering personal growth and social mobility, and plays a critical role in shaping communities. Shaping inclusive and equitable communities involves deliberate selection, design, and development of information and delivery models. We explore topics related to teaching and learning, including Bloom's Taxonomy of Learning, adult education strategies, defining coherent life objectives, individualized mission, vision, and values in learning objectives, and eliminating metacognitive dissonance in teaching and learning. These topics can help us to develop a deeper understanding of the importance of education and its impact on individuals, societies, and nations. This is a book about designing the future.

"Homines dum docent discunt"

-Seneca

PART 1

DEFINING EDUCATION

Education is getting knowledge, skills, and development through study or practice. It is the field of study that deals with the methods and challenges of teaching.

There are different forms of education, including formal education (such as schooling), informal education (such as learning from experience), and self-education (such as learning through reading and research). Education can provide academic, practical, and social expertise. The general goal of education is to help students learn and grow. This includes helping them acquire knowledge and skills and develop unique talents and abilities.

The four pillars of education are:

1. Learning to know.

This is acquiring the fundamental knowledge and skills needed for individual and collective development. It includes learning how to learn, how to think critically, and how to solve problems.

2. **Learning to do.**

This is the active acquiring of the practical skills and knowledge needed for employment and social participation. It includes knowing how to use technology, work with others, and manage oneself.

3. **Learning to live together.**

This means developing the ability to live peacefully and harmoniously with others, regardless of their differences. It includes learning about different cultures, how to resolve conflict, and how to build relationships.

4. **Learning to be.**

Which is working to realize one's full potential. This means developing one's unique talents and abilities and becoming well-rounded. It includes learning about self, setting goals, and achieving one's full potential.

Education is a complex and ever-changing field, and there is no one-size-fits-all approach to teaching. However, the goal of education is always the same:

"To help students learn and grow."

These four pillars are essential for preparing all people for the challenges of the future. They provide a framework for education that is relevant, engaging, and effective.

Rethinking the Design of Education

It is helpful to rethink our educational system design around three levels of knowledge and skills. This can be a helpful approach to help students develop a more holistic understanding of any subject matter. The three levels are foundational knowledge and skills, application knowledge and skills, and synthesizing knowledge and skills.

Foundational knowledge and skills:

This level encompasses the basic concepts and skills

necessary to understand a subject. This includes facts, theories, and principles that form the foundation of the subject. For example, in math, this might consist of learning basic arithmetic operations, algebra, and geometry. It might include learning about the scientific method and basic scientific concepts in science. In writing begins with memorizing the alphabet and working through the rules of grammar.

Application knowledge and skills:

This level involves applying the foundational knowledge and skills to real-world situations. Students should learn how to use what they have learned in real-life scenarios. This can include problem-solving, critical thinking, and decision-making skills. In math, this might involve solving real-world math problems. In contrast, it might consist of conducting experiments and analyzing data in science. In writing, this can be applied to research and analysis of complex ideas.

Synthesizing knowledge and skills:

This level combines foundational and applied knowledge and skills to create new insights, ideas, and solutions. This is the highest level of learning, where students demonstrate their ability to think critically, innovate, and create new ideas. In math, this might involve creating a new mathematical formula. In contrast, science might include designing a new experiment or proposing a new theory. In writing this can be creating and expressing innovative and novel ideas.

By incorporating all three levels of learning into educational system design, students can develop a deeper understanding of a subject and be better equipped to apply their knowledge and skills in the real world. Foundational knowledge and skills are essential for learning and success in many life areas. This includes basic skills such as arithmetic, reading, comprehension, and the ability to follow instructions, as well as fundamental concepts and principles that underpin many different fields of study.

However, it's also essential to include an understanding of how to learn as a foundational skill. This involves developing metacognitive skills or thinking about and monitoring one's learning process. Students who understand how to learn can better set goals, plan their learning, and evaluate their progress. This is metacognition. Foundational skills are applicable across all academic disciplines.

Essential Metacognitive Skills

Some essential metacognitive skills include:

Self-assessment: The ability to accurately assess one's knowledge and skills and identify areas for improvement.

Goal-setting: The ability to set specific, measurable, achievable, relevant, and time-bound (SMART) goals for learning.

Planning: The ability to create a plan for achieving learning goals, including identifying resources and strategies for learning.

Monitoring: The ability to monitor one's progress toward learning goals and make adjustments as needed.

Reflection: The ability to reflect on one's own learning, including identifying successes and challenges and using this information to inform future learning.

Educators can help students become more effective and efficient learners and better equipped to succeed in academic and professional settings by including an understanding of how to learn as a foundational skill. Educators play a critical role in shaping their students' learning experiences, and understanding how to learn is essential for their success as teachers.

Here are some reasons why educators must understand this concept:

To help students become better learners: By understanding how to learn, educators can help their students become more effective and efficient learners. This can lead to better academic performance and increased motivation to learn.

To personalize learning: Every student has unique learning styles and preferences. By understanding how to learn, educators can personalize their teaching to meet the needs of individual students and help them achieve their learning goals.

To foster a growth mindset: Students who understand how to learn are likelier to develop a growth mindset, believing that intelligence and abilities can be acquired through hard work and dedication. Educators who understand this concept can help foster their students' growth mindset and promote a lifelong learning culture.

To promote metacognitive skills: Metacognitive skills are essential for effective learning but are not always explicitly taught in schools. Educators who understand how to learn can expressly teach these skills to their students, helping them become more self-aware and reflective learners.

To support the development of skills for the future: In today's rapidly changing world, students need to develop a range of skills beyond academic knowledge, including critical thinking, problem-solving, and collaboration. Educators who understand how to learn can help their students develop these 21st-century skills essential for success in the workforce and in life.

Overall, understanding how to learn is essential for educators to be effective in their teaching and support the success of their students.

Metacognitive Dissonance

Without foundational knowledge, there are no

foundational skills. For example, I have seen billboards promoting Stroke awareness. The billboard states, "At the first sign of a stroke, dial 911." The intention of the message is clear; however, people lacking knowledge about strokes realize no benefits from this campaign. To make this message valid, the educator-marketer should define a stroke, tell why it is crucial, and provide a list of the symptoms.

Without the required knowledge to support an experience, one will sense discomfort and infidelity when attempting to understand the experience. This infidelity is cognitive dissonance and a mental blind spot. This cognitive gap is sometimes satisfied with propaganda and dogmatic doctrines of different types *-the burden of ignorance.* People who accept ideas without understanding their basis, might be responding to the "Herd mentality." This means they are taking cues from the environment because they seem to satisfy the void of ignorance. People are attempting to resolve a metacognitive dissonance.

Metacognitive dissonance is a term used to describe the mental discomfort or conflict that arises when a person's beliefs, thoughts, or attitudes about their own thinking or cognitive processes are challenged or contradicted by new information. It is essentially a form of cognitive dissonance that occurs at a higher level of thinking, where an individual's beliefs about their own thinking processes clash with the actual performance of those processes.

For example, if someone believes they are very good at solving math problems but then struggles to solve a complex one, they may experience metacognitive dissonance. This is because the evidence of their actual performance is contradicting their belief about their thinking ability.

Metacognitive dissonance can also arise when people encounter information that challenges their beliefs about how they learn or remember information. For example, if someone believes they are good at memorizing information but then struggles to recall information during a test, they may experience metacognitive dissonance.

The discomfort from metacognitive dissonance can motivate people to re-evaluate their beliefs about their thinking processes and make changes to improve their cognitive abilities. However, if the discomfort is too substantial, it may lead to avoidance of challenging tasks or a reluctance to confront new information that contradicts one's beliefs about their own thinking abilities.

Metacognitive dissonance is a form of cognitive dissonance that occurs when a person's beliefs about their own thinking processes clash with the evidence of their actual performance. It can be a motivating force for personal growth and improvement. Still, it can also lead to avoidance and reluctance if the discomfort is too intense. We have collective metacognitive dissonance in education. Much of our current ideas and position about education reflects metacognitive dissonance. We are convinced we understand the problem and have solutions, but data shows we are consistently underperforming.

We must admit that we have a problem before we can begin the heavy lifting required to find and implement the solution.

PART 2

HEALTHY EDUCATIONAL BUREAUCRACY

Administration in Education

Administrators play a critical role in education, providing leadership, vision, and support for teachers and students. Here are some key roles and responsibilities of administrators in education:

Setting the vision and direction: Administrators are responsible for setting the vision and direction for their schools or districts. This involves developing and communicating a clear mission statement and goals, ensuring all stakeholders are aligned, and working towards common objectives.

Providing instructional leadership:
Administrators are responsible for providing instructional leadership to their teachers. This involves setting high

expectations for teaching and learning, providing professional development opportunities, and ensuring all students access high-quality instruction.

Managing resources: Administrators are responsible for managing the help of their schools or districts, including budgets, facilities, and staffing. This involves making strategic decisions about resource allocation to support the school or district's goals. In adult education, this focus should be the learners' goal. It is helpful to remember that students are the purpose of the job and not protecting the policies and rules.

Ensuring compliance with regulations: Administrators are responsible for ensuring that their schools or districts comply with all relevant rules and policies. This includes federal, state, and local laws and district policies and procedures.

Supporting teachers and staff: Administrators are responsible for supporting their teachers and staff's professional development and well-being. This includes providing opportunities for growth and development, recognizing and celebrating accomplishments, and creating a positive and supportive work environment.

Building relationships with stakeholders:
Administrators are responsible for building positive
relationships with stakeholders, including parents,
community members, and other organizations. This
involves effective communication, collaboration, and
engagement to ensure all stakeholders work towards
common goals.

Overall, administrators play a critical role in
education, providing leadership, vision, and support for
teachers and students to ensure that all students have
access to high-quality instruction and the support they
need to succeed. As the world changes and new
challenges emerge, it's important to continually rethink
and innovate the education administration to ensure that
schools and districts meet all learners' needs.

**Here are some potential areas for rethinking
the administration of education:**

Emphasizing a culture of collaboration: In many
schools and districts, there can be a hierarchical or siloed

approach to administration, with little cooperation between different departments or levels. However, a culture of collaboration can help ensure that everyone is working towards common goals and actively listening to the opinions of all stakeholders. Administrators can foster this culture by providing opportunities for collaboration, such as team meetings, professional development sessions, and joint projects.

Using data to inform decision-making: In today's data-driven world, administrators can use data to inform decision-making and drive improvements in instruction and student outcomes. This can involve collecting and analyzing data on student performance, teacher effectiveness, and resource allocation and using this information to make data-informed decisions about teaching, learning, and administration.

Supporting innovation and experimentation: Education is constantly evolving, and administrators can support innovation and experiment to find new and effective ways of teaching and learning. This can involve providing opportunities for teachers to try new approaches and techniques, encouraging experimentation with new technologies, and supporting research and development initiatives.

Prioritizing equity and inclusivity:
Administrators have a critical role in promoting equity and inclusivity in education. This involves ensuring that all students have access to high-quality instruction, resources, and support. Also, working to meet the needs of diverse learners. Administrators can prioritize equity and inclusivity by examining and addressing biases in policies and practices, fostering a culture of inclusivity, and providing targeted support for underrepresented students.

Embracing technology: Technology is increasingly vital in education, and administrators can embrace this trend to support teaching and learning. This can involve providing resources and support for teachers to integrate technology into their instruction, using technology to streamline administrative tasks, and leveraging data and analytics to support decision-making.

By rethinking education administration in these and other areas, administrators can help ensure that schools provide high-quality instruction and support to all learners and are prepared for future challenges.

PART 3

READING, COMPREHENSION, AND FOLLOWING INSTRUCTION

Understanding the Basics in Education

Reading, comprehension, and the ability to follow instructions are crucial skills that can significantly impact an individual's personal and professional success. We can easily visualize the nightmarish existence of cars, trucks, and all types of transportation on a system of roads without rules.

Why this Matters

Improved Communication: Reading helps improve communication skills, including writing and speaking. By reading extensively, individuals can gain a broader vocabulary, better understand grammar, and learn how to express themselves effectively. This, in turn, can enhance their ability to communicate with others, convey ideas and thoughts clearly, and understand others' points of view. This means reading is a facet of emotional, social, relationship, cultural, and general intelligence.

Enhanced Comprehension: Comprehension is understanding the meaning of words, phrases, and paragraphs. This produces coherency in thoughts and the interpretation of stimuli. Strong comprehension skills help individuals read and understand complex texts, including academic and technical materials, which are essential in the professional world. Additionally, strong comprehension skills enable individuals to analyze and synthesize information for making informed decisions. A low level of comprehension produces intellectual handicaps.

Increased Productivity: Following instructions is essential in personal and professional life. Following instructions accurately and efficiently can help people complete tasks and projects on time, avoid mistakes, and increase productivity. For example, in a professional setting, following instructions from a supervisor or manager can help employees complete their assigned tasks accurately, meet deadlines, and avoid costly errors.

Improved Learning: Reading and comprehension skills are vital for learning and education. Individuals who read and comprehend well are likelier to excel in public life and school, absorb new information quickly, and succeed. Additionally, reading can help individuals broaden their knowledge, gain new perspectives, and develop critical thinking skills essential for personal growth and development.

Therefore, reading, comprehension, and the ability to follow instructions are crucial skills that can significantly impact an individual's personal and professional success. These skills help individuals communicate effectively, understand complex ideas, increase productivity, and improve learning. By developing these skills, individuals can position themselves for success in all areas of life.

Low or No Ability to Read, Comprehend, and Follow Instructions

Low or no ability to read, comprehend, and follow instructions creates a multilayer handicap experience. Because it can significantly impact an individual's social and professional well-being.

Potential impacts can include:

Limited Job Opportunities: In today's competitive job market, employers often require employees to have basic reading and comprehension skills and the ability to follow instructions accurately. Individuals who lack these skills may find it challenging to secure employment, limiting their job opportunities and career growth.

Difficulty in Communication: Low reading and comprehension skills can hinder communication with others, making it difficult to understand instructions, follow conversations, or express oneself clearly. This can lead to frustration, misunderstandings, and social isolation.

Reduced Self-Confidence: The inability to read, comprehend, and follow instructions can lead to low self-esteem and lowered self-confidence. Individuals who struggle with these skills may feel inadequate and discouraged, affecting their mental health and overall well-being.

Limited Access to Information: Reading and comprehension skills are essential for accessing information and knowledge. Without these skills, one may struggle to keep up with current events, access educational resources, or understand crucial documents such as contracts or legal papers.

Limited Life Opportunities: Low reading and comprehension skills can limit an individual's ability to participate in everyday activities such as grocery shopping, paying bills, or voting. This can profoundly impact an individual's overall quality of life.

Exaggerated emotional and mental stress and physiological harm.

Subjected to manipulation: Illiteracy creates a

population that is easier to manipulate. It does not take much to imagine which unscrupulous group depends on ignorance.

Hence, low or no ability to read, comprehend, and follow instructions can profoundly impact an individual's social and professional well-being. It can limit job opportunities, hinder communication, reduce self-confidence, limit access to information, limit life opportunities, and increase harmful stress. Therefore, developing and strengthening these skills is essential to succeed in all areas of life.

The apparent challenge one might experience with these challenges produces the sense of being trapped within the confines of intellectual darkness. Overcoming this type of challenge requires external support.

Causes of Illiteracy
Illiteracy refers to the inability to read or write. It can have various causes, including:

Lack of Access to Education: One of the primary causes of illiteracy is the lack of access to education. In some parts of the world, particular population segments may not have access to schools, teachers, or educational materials. This can be due to poverty, geographic isolation, cultural barriers, or government policies.

Poverty: Poverty is another significant cause of illiteracy. Many impoverished families cannot afford to send their children to school or provide them with educational resources. Additionally, poverty can force children to work instead of attending school, limiting their access to education.

Cultural Barriers: Cultural barriers such as gender, race, ethnicity, and religion can also contribute to illiteracy. In some cultures, girls may not have access to education, or some ethnic or religious groups may face discrimination or limited education opportunities.

Learning Disabilities: Learning disabilities such as dyslexia can also contribute to illiteracy. Individuals with learning disabilities may struggle with reading or writing, even with access to education and resources.

Migration: Migration and displacement can also contribute to illiteracy. When individuals are forced to leave their homes and communities, they may not have access to education or face language barriers that hinder their learning ability.

Health Issues: Health issues like malnutrition, poor health care, and diseases like HIV/AIDS can also contribute to illiteracy. Children who suffer from malnutrition or poor health may not have the physical or cognitive ability to learn, and illnesses such as HIV/AIDS can affect brain development and cognitive functioning.

The causes of illiteracy are complex and multifaceted, including lack of access to education, poverty, cultural barriers, learning disabilities, migration, and health issues. Addressing these causes requires a comprehensive approach that includes improving access to education, reducing poverty, promoting inclusivity and diversity, and addressing health issues. Such efforts are crucial in reducing illiteracy and promoting overall development and well-being.

Measuring Literacy
There are various ways to measure levels of literacy.

Here are some commonly used methods:

Standardized Tests: Standardized tests are a common way to measure literacy levels. These tests assess reading, writing, and comprehension skills and provide a standardized measure of an individual's literacy level. Examples of standardized tests include the National Assessment of Adult Literacy (NAAL) in the United States and the Program for the International Assessment of Adult Competencies (PIAAC) in other countries.

Self-Reporting: Self-reporting is another method used to measure literacy levels. This method involves individuals self-reporting their literacy level using surveys or questionnaires. Self-reporting can provide a general idea of an individual's literacy level. Still, it may be subject to bias or inaccuracies.

Functional Literacy Assessments: Functional literacy assessments measure an individual's ability to use literacy skills in practical situations, such as understanding instructions, filling out forms, or reading labels. These assessments provide a more realistic measure of an individual's literacy level. They can help identify specific areas where support is needed.

Observational Assessments: Observational assessments involve observing an individual's literacy skills in real-life situations, such as in the workplace or school. These assessments can provide a more accurate picture of an individual's literacy level in specific contexts.

Informal Assessments: Informal assessments involve informal measures, such as conversations or informal writing samples, to evaluate an individual's literacy level. While not as standardized as other methods, valid and reliable assessments can provide valuable insights into an individual's literacy level and specific areas where support may be needed.

Various methods exist to measure literacy levels, including standardized tests, self-reporting, functional literacy assessments, observational assessments, and informal assessments. While the choice of method depends on the specific context and purpose of the evaluation, the ability to measure is a vital step toward resolving the challenge. We can fix or repair only what we can measure.

PART 4

LITERACY

Functional Literacy

Functionally literate refers to an individual's ability to use their literacy skills in practical, real-life situations. It goes beyond the ability to simply read and write to encompass the ability to understand, analyze, and apply information from written materials in everyday life situations.

Being functionally literate means an individual can read and understand instructions, fill out forms, read labels, use technology, and communicate effectively in writing. It also involves critical thinking skills, such as analyzing and evaluating information and applying it to solve problems or make decisions.

Functionally literate individuals are better

equipped to navigate the demands of modern society, such as finding and maintaining employment, managing finances, and accessing healthcare. They will likely participate in lifelong learning, pursue higher education, and participate in civic activities.

The concept of functional literacy is particularly relevant in adult literacy, where the focus is not just on essential reading and writing skills but on developing practical literacy skills that can improve an individual's quality of life and increase their participation in society. This conversation addresses general literacy but recognizes there are other important areas like financial literacy.

Role of Teachers in Learning

As educators, teachers need to have a solid understanding of how people learn.

Here are some key concepts that a teacher should know about learning:

Learning is an Active Process: Learning is not passive; it requires active engagement from the learner. Teachers should design learning experiences encouraging students to actively engage with the material through discussion, problem-solving, and hands-on activities.

Learning is Constructive: People construct their understanding of the world through their experiences, and this understanding is constantly evolving. Teachers should recognize that students come to the classroom with pre-existing knowledge and beliefs and build upon that knowledge to create new learning experiences.

Learning is Social: People learn from each other through social interaction, collaboration, and feedback. Teachers should create opportunities for students to collaborate, share ideas, and receive constructive feedback.

Teachers who understand the science of learning can create environments where students can be successful. One standard model is Bloom's Taxonomy of Learning.

Blooms Taxonomy of Learning

Bloom's Taxonomy is a hierarchical model that defines educational goals and objectives into six cognitive levels of complexity. It was developed by educational psychologist Benjamin Bloom and his colleagues in 1956 and has been revised several times since then.

The six levels are:

Remembering: This level involves recalling or recognizing previously learned information. Examples of tasks at this level include listing, naming, and defining.

Understanding: This level emphasizes comprehending the meaning of the information. Examples of tasks at this level include summarizing, explaining, and interpreting.

Applying: This level involves using the information in a new or different situation. Examples of tasks at this level include using, executing, and implementing.

Analyzing: This level involves breaking down information into components and identifying relationships among the parts. Examples of tasks at this level include comparing, contrasting, and categorizing.

Evaluating: This level focuses on making judgments about the value or quality of the information.

Examples of tasks at this level include evaluating, assessing, and critiquing.

Creating: This level involves using the information to create something new. Examples of tasks at this level include designing, constructing, and developing.

The levels build on each other, requiring mastery of the preceding level. Educators often use Bloom's Taxonomy to develop and structure learning objectives, design assessment tasks, and plan instructional activities. Using Bloom's Taxonomy, educators can ensure that students learn at a level appropriate for their abilities and gradually build their skills and knowledge.

PART 5

UNDERSTANDING ADULT EDUCATION STRATEGIES

Adult in Education

Adult education is the practice of providing educational opportunities for adults who are beyond the traditional age for formal education. It involves many programs, courses, and learning activities designed to meet adult learners' unique needs and interests.

Some common strategies used in adult education include:

Needs Assessment: Conducting a needs assessment is essential in determining what topics and skills adults need to learn. This assessment helps in designing and developing relevant educational programs.

Learner-Centered Approach: Adult education should be tailored to the learner's needs. Adult learners often have unique life experiences and circumstances that must be considered. Therefore, a learner-centered approach ensures that the learner's needs are considered in the learning process.

Experiential Learning: This approach focuses on learning through experience, allowing adults to learn by doing. Experiential learning often involves hands-on activities, simulations, and problem-based learning.

Collaborative Learning: Collaborative learning involves learning in a group setting, where individuals work together to solve problems or complete tasks. This approach fosters social interaction, which is essential in adult learning.

Blended Learning: Blended learning merges typical face-to-face instruction with online or remote learning. This approach allows learners to access materials and resources anytime and anywhere.

Flexible learning: Adults have many responsibilities, including work, family, and other commitments. Flexible learning allows adult learners to fit their studies around these responsibilities through online courses, evening classes, and self-paced learning materials.

Prior learning assessment and recognition (PLAR): Many adult learners gain valuable knowledge and skills from work and life experiences. PLAR allows these learners to have their prior learning recognized, so they can receive credit toward a formal qualification.

Problem-based learning: This approach focuses on real-life problems and issues, encouraging learners to think critically and solve problems. It is often used in professional development programs for adult learners, such as in healthcare or business.

Collaborative learning: Many adult learners prefer to work in groups or teams, and collaborative learning provides group work and discussion opportunities. This can help to build communication skills and develop teamwork abilities.

Mentoring and coaching: Adult learners may benefit from one-to-one support and guidance from a mentor or coach. This can help to build confidence, provide personalized feedback, and support the development of new skills.

Personalized learning plans: Many adult learners have specific goals and interests, and customized learning plans can help them to achieve these goals. These plans are developed collaboratively between the learner and the educator, providing a roadmap for success.

Overall, adult education strategies should be learner-centered, recognize adult learners' diverse needs and experiences, and be designed to support learners in achieving their goals and advancing their careers. Adult learners who function below the expected academic level for their age can have emotional hurdles to navigate in the learning process. Therefore, teachers and coaches must demonstrate patience and respect to reinforce confidence and provide encouragement.

Adult Learners Roles and Learning Objectives

Assisting learners in defining coherent life objectives is essential to adult education because solving challenges one cannot visualize is difficult.

Here are some strategies that can help:

Goal Setting: Encourage learners to set SMART goals (Specific, Measurable, Attainable, Relevant, Time-bound) aligned with their values and interests. This will help them to clarify their priorities and create a roadmap for achieving their objectives.

Self-Assessment: Encourage learners to reflect on their strengths, weaknesses, and areas for improvement. This can help them to identify the relevant and applicable skills and knowledge they need to achieve their goals and to develop a plan for acquiring these skills.

Values Clarification: Help learners to identify their core values and beliefs and to align their life goals with these values. This can help them to achieve a sense of purpose and meaning in their lives.

Career Exploration: Help learners to explore different career options and to identify the skills and qualifications needed for these careers. This can help them to choose a career path in fidelity to their interests and values.

Support Networks: Encourage learners to build a support network of friends, family members, and mentors who can provide guidance and support as they work towards their life objectives.

Action Planning: Help learners to create a detailed action plan that outlines the steps they need to take to achieve their life objectives. This can include setting deadlines, identifying resources, and developing strategies for overcoming obstacles.

Helping learners define coherent life objectives requires a holistic approach that addresses their personal, professional, and educational goals. By providing learners with the tools and support they need to achieve their dreams, adult educators can help learners to reach their full potential and lead fulfilling lives. Think of these as identifying the compelling reason for the students to learn.

PART 6

MISSION, VISION, AND VALUES IN LEARNING OBJECTIVES

Outcome Based Learning

Individualized mission, vision, and values can be incorporated into learning objectives to help learners connect their personal goals and values to their educational pursuits.

Here are some strategies for doing so:

Personal Mission Statement: Encourage learners to develop a personal mission statement that reflects their core values and beliefs. This statement can serve as a guiding principle for their educational pursuits and can be integrated into learning objectives.

Vision Statement: Help learners to develop a vision statement that outlines their long-term goals and aspirations. This statement can help them stay focused on their objectives and can be used to create learning objectives aligned with their vision.

Values Alignment: Help learners to identify their values and to align their educational goals with these values. This can help them stay motivated and engaged in their studies. It can be reflected in learning objectives emphasizing developing skills and knowledge that align with their values.

Self-Reflection: Encourage learners to think about what they are learning and experiencing and identify how their values and goals have influenced their educational pursuits. This can help them develop learning objectives aligned with their mission and vision.

Individualized Learning Plans: Help learners to create individualized learning plans that reflect their personal goals, values, and learning preferences. This can help ensure that learning objectives are tailored to the individual learner's needs.

Incorporating individualized mission, vision, and values into learning objectives can help learners to connect their educational pursuits to their personal goals and values. This can increase motivation, engagement, and satisfaction with the learning process and help learners achieve their full potential.

Measuring Success in Teaching and Learning

Measuring success in teaching and learning is vital to ensure that learners meet their educational objectives and identify areas for improvement in the teaching and learning process.

Here are some common strategies for measuring success:

Assessment: Assessments can be used to measure learning outcomes and to evaluate the effectiveness of the teaching and learning process. This can include tests, quizzes, assignments, projects, and other forms of assessment that measure student knowledge and skills.

Rubrics: Rubrics can provide clear expectations for learning outcomes and evaluate student work against specific criteria. This can help ensure that assessments align with learning objectives and that grading is consistent and fair.

Surveys and Feedback: Surveys and feedback can be used to gather information from learners about their experiences with the teaching and learning process. This can include feedback on the quality of instruction, the effectiveness of learning materials, and the overall learning experience.

Reflection and Self-Assessment: Reflection and self-assessment can be used by learners to evaluate their own learning progress and to identify areas for improvement. This can help to promote self-directed learning and can be used to inform future learning objectives.

Program Evaluation: Evaluations can be used to assess the overall effectiveness of a teaching and learning program. This can include gathering data on student outcomes, teacher performance, and the program's impact on learners and the community.

Follow-Up: Follow-up can be used to assess the long-term impact of the teaching and learning process on learners. This can include gathering data on how learners apply their knowledge and skills in real-life settings and evaluating their success in achieving their career and personal goals.

Measuring success in teaching and learning requires a comprehensive approach that includes a range of assessment strategies and methods. The best teachers are competent in their subject areas and are emotionally mature. By using these strategies, educators can ensure that learners are meeting their educational objectives and can continually improve the teaching and learning process.

Who Benefits from Education and Literacy

Education and literacy benefit individuals, societies, and nations in various ways.

Here are some of the key benefits:

Personal Development: Education and literacy can contribute to personal development by expanding knowledge and skills, building confidence and self-esteem, and promoting critical thinking and problem-solving abilities.

Career Opportunities: Education and literacy can increase employment opportunities and earning potential by providing individuals with the knowledge and skills needed in professional life.

Social Mobility: Education and literacy can promote social mobility by providing individuals with the knowledge and skills to succeed in higher education and professional careers.

Health and Well-being: Education and literacy can contribute to better health outcomes by promoting health literacy, enabling people to make informed health decisions, and reducing the incidence of chronic diseases.

Democratic Participation: Education and literacy can promote democratic participation by enabling individuals to understand and engage in political processes and exercise their rights and responsibilities as citizens. Many repressive regimes suppress education in the general population.

Economic Growth: Education and literacy can contribute to economic growth by increasing productivity, promoting innovation and entrepreneurship, and attracting investment and business development.

Social Cohesion: Education and literacy can promote social cohesion by fostering understanding and tolerance of different cultures and perspectives and building social capital through networks and community involvement.

Overall, education and literacy have broad and far-reaching benefits that extend beyond the individual to benefit society. Individuals, organizations, and nations can work towards more significant social, economic, and political development and progress by promoting education and literacy. Access to basic education is a human right. It is also how societies can demonstrate equity, inclusion, and tolerance for people of diverse backgrounds.

Conclusion

The concepts we have covered are all important parts of a whole that is education. Having a strategic approach that uses a scientific approach to teaching and learning can improve the probability of a positive result. A strategic approach allows for a clear direction and goal, while a scientific approach ensures that the teaching and learning methods used are evidence-based and effective. Passion, competence, and service are all important aspects of effective teaching and learning.

Passion allows for a love of learning and a desire to share that love with others. Competence ensures that the teacher is knowledgeable and skilled in the subject matter being taught. Service means that the teacher is committed to the success of their students and willing to go above and beyond to ensure that they are successful. When passion, competence, and service overlap, they produce a sense of purpose that is greater than any individual goal. This purpose is about creating a world where academic inclusion is the norm and where everyone has access to the resources and support, they need to succeed. It is about pushing back against the boundaries of exclusion and working to minimize the impacts of mental stress, anxiety, low testing results, and artificial stratification in society.

By adopting a strategic and scientific approach to teaching and learning, and by prioritizing passion, competence, and service, we can work towards a more inclusive and equitable society where everyone can reach their full potential.

The End.

PART 7

SOURCES

Some specific sources used in this book accessed with chatGPT and BARD AI include:
Textbooks and academic articles on education and learning theory.

Online learning platforms and educational websites like EdX, Coursera, and Khan Academy.

Government reports and statistical data on education, such as the National Center for Education Statistics in the United States.

Research studies on various topics related to education and learning, such as cognitive psychology, adult education, and teaching strategies.

Educational experts and practitioners, including educators, trainers, and instructional designers.

Conferences, seminars, and workshops on education and learning.

Online forums and discussion groups where educators and learners share their experiences and perspectives on various educational topics.

These sources provide a diverse range of perspectives and insights into the field of education, allowing for a comprehensive and multidimensional understanding of the topics discussed.

Darling-Hammond, L., LaPointe, M., Meyerson, D., Orr,

M. T., & Cohen, C. (2009). Preparing school leaders for a changing world: Lessons from exemplary leadership development programs. Stanford, CA: Stanford Educational Leadership Institute.

Flavell, J. H. (1979). Metacognition and cognitive monitoring: A new area of cognitive-developmental inquiry. American Psychologist, 34(10), 906-911.

Fullan, M. (2014). The principal: Three keys to maximizing impact. San Francisco, CA: Jossey-Bass.

Halverson, R., Grigg, J., Prichett, R., & Thomas, C. (2015). The new instructional leadership: Creating data-driven instructional systems in schools. Journal of School Leadership, 25(6), 1106-1129.

Hargreaves, A., & Fink, D. (2006). Sustainable leadership. San Francisco, CA: Jossey-Bass.

Kruglanski, A. W., & Stroebe, W. (Eds.). (2005). Handbook of the history of social psychology. Sage Publications.

Kunda, Z. (1999). Social cognition: Making sense of people. MIT Press.

Leithwood, K., & Mascall, B. (2008). Collective leadership effects on student achievement. Educational Administration Quarterly, 44(4), 529-561.

Schraw, G., & Dennison, R. S. (1994). Assessing metacognitive awareness. Contemporary Educational Psychology, 19(4), 460-475.

33995635R00036